# MEZE

SMALL PLATES TO SAVOR AND SHARE FROM THE MEDITERRANEAN TABLE

DIANE KOCHILAS *

WILLIAM MORROW

An Imprint of HarperCollinsPublishers

OTHER BOOKS BY THE AUTHOR

*The Glorious Foods of Greece*
*The Greek Vegetarian*
*The Food and Wine of Greece*

HarperCollins books may be purchased for educational, business, or sales promotional use.
For information please write:
Special Markets Department, HarperCollins Publishers Inc., 10 East 53rd Street, New York, NY 10022.

FIRST EDITION

*Designed by Platinum Design, Inc. NYC*

*Photographs by Melanie Acevedo*
*Food styling by Corinne Trang*
*Prop styling by Kathleen Hackett*

Printed on acid-free paper

Library of Congress Cataloging-in-Publication Data

Kochilas, Diane.
Meze: Small Plates to Savor and Share from the Mediterranean Table / Diane Kochilas.—1st ed.
p. cm.
ISBN 0-688-17511-2
1. Appetizers—Greece. 2. Cookery, Greek. I. Title.
TX740 K635 2003
641.8'12'09495—dc21
2002032881

03 04 05 06 07 ❖/IM 10 9 8 7 6 5 4 3 2 1

FOR YIORGOS AND KYVELI—I HOPE THEIR LIVES ARE ALWAYS FILLED

WITH GOOD THINGS TO SAVOR AND GOOD PEOPLE TO SHARE THEM WITH

✳

CONTENTS

ACKNOWLEDGMENTS IX

MEZE CULTURE—AN INTRODUCTION X

✳

ACKNOWLEDGMENTS

I shared more than a few plates with friends, family, and colleagues while cooking meze feasts.

Harriet Bell, my editor, made *Meze* a feast to savor by spicing it up in all the right directions and parring it down wisely in others. Melanie Acevedo, photographer par excellence, made *Meze* a feast for the eyes. Doe Coover, my agent and friend, is always deserving of accolades for sharing advice and standing by during the highs and lows.

I owe special thanks to my friend and fellow cook, Brigitte Bernhardt Fatsio, who tested the recipes and offered up a few of her own for me to enjoy and pass along. I'd also like to thank Lefteris Lazarou, chef-owner of Greece's Michelin-starred seafood restaurant Varoulko, for opening his recipe files and sharing more than a few tricks of the trade. Special thanks to Sotiris Bafitis, a passionate Greek wine specialist, who helped me figure out what kinds of wine go best with mezethes.

The book's designer, Platinum Design, seasoned *Meze* with great visual taste, and Sonia Greenbaum proved that copyediting, like cooking, is a detail-lover's art. Thanks!

Finally, I always owe special thanks to my husband, Vassilis Stenos, a willing partner in conviviality and an able judge of what's good and what's not. I will always be grateful for having a loving family with whom it's always a joy to savor and share every last morsel.

# MEZE CULTURE—
# AN INTRODUCTION

When I moved to Greece ten years ago, I had to switch gears from the frenzied pace of New York City to the more relaxed rhythms of the Mediterranean. I moved to Athens, a chaotic, bustling city whose charms take some time to uncover. One of the things I loved from the very start though was something I used to joke about, granted, with a little bit of New York sarcasm—that in the middle of every afternoon, throngs of people of working age, men and women alike from every walk of life, were crowded around small tables all over the city, clinking glasses, sharing plates, talking loudly in that lively, excessive way Greeks have when discussing . . . everything. They were doing what people in this part of the world have been doing for literally thousands of years—partaking in the trinity of food, drink, and dialogue (not always in that order), relaxing and socializing over a glass or two of wine or beer or ouzo and some savory tidbits of food. I was witnessing meze culture firsthand. It seemed much more civilized than "doing" lunch New York style.

In the eastern Mediterranean, there are special restaurants where you can go to savor mezethes. In Greece, they even have various names. There is the *mezethopoleion*, or general meze restaurant; the *ouzeri*, or ouzo restaurant; and the *tsipouradiko* or *rakadiko*—where people go for Greek eau-de-vie, called *tsipouro* or raki. A mezethopoleion might have slightly more substantial fare on the menu, and a bona fide wine list. Ouzo and Greek raki haunts tend to offer more piquant food, specifically designed to match strong liqueurs.

This way of eating—or rather socializing—was not entirely new to me when I moved to Greece. I grew up in a Greek family in New York, and on many afternoons or early evenings we had guests at our kitchen table, friends of the family who would come by unannounced and stay to chat for an hour, maybe for two or three. It went without saying that my parents, as hosts, even ad hoc ones, offered them a little something to drink—it might have been anything from coffee (an American habit they co-opted, but always with a food spin) to a scotch, to some Metaxa brandy, or ouzo, or wine—and with it something small to eat: bread or *paximathia* (rusks), olives, cheese, maybe a small bowl of taramosalata, if there happened to be some in the house, or maybe just a quartered tomato and sliced cucumber. These simple foods are the basics of the meze table.

The idea of food as a pretext for socializing is unique to the Mediterranean, and especially to the ancient eastern Mediterranean, in countries such as Greece, Turkey, Lebanon, and others. Although meze cuisine belongs to the general tradition of dining on a variety of dishes at once—on small plates, so to speak— meze culture is not akin to Spanish tapas or to French hors d'oeuvres or to Italian antipasti.

*Mezethes* (plural of meze) are not appetizers, and never immediately precede a main meal. Greeks have appetizers, too. They call them *orektika*. Mezethes are different.

The words *meze, mezze, maza, meza* mean middle, as in middle of the day or between lunch and dinner. Mezethes are almost always meant to play second fiddle to the drink at hand. In Middle Eastern countries, that would mostly be arak. In Greece, where there is a long history of viticulture, there are mezethes that are meant to accompany wines and others that match better with stronger drinks, such as ouzo and tsipouro or raki (arak). In general, mezethes meant for strong liqueurs tend to be robust and spicy; those that are meant to complement wine are generally a little milder. But there is no hard-and-fast rule. It isn't taboo to have both wine and ouzo or raki on the table.

The most important aspect of meze is that it is a cuisine meant not to sate but to tease. The whole point of snacking this way is to make the experience at table last as long as possible. The main reason for being around the meze table is to talk, to share thoughts with a few friends over a glass or two of wine or liqueur and something to eat.

Eating this way is a kind of game, and a civilized one at that, my good friend and culinary pundit (he's the Brillat-Savarin of Greece)

Christos Zouraris once told me. Savoring mezethes requires a certain discipline, precisely because you are not supposed to fill your belly as you would at a full-fledged lunch or dinner. "Invite three friends around a table. Place a well-appointed plate filled with four Kalamata olives, four hot pickled peppers, two salted sardines cut in half, and two slices of bread, also cut in two, and one bottle of the appropriate wine or good ouzo. If you can manage to keep your friends there for an hour, drinking, nibbling, and talking, then you have mastered the game." So he suggests in an essay he wrote on the subject about a decade ago.

✳

There is an element of ritual in the meze tradition. In the small provincial port city of Volos, for example, within proximity of some of the best ouzo and tsipouro makers in the country, meze dining has evolved into a specific way to eat, so much so that in other parts of Greece restaurants open boasting Volos-style meze dining. The meze experience here follows a certain order, indelibly linked to imbibing, which is part of the whole experience no matter where one happens to be. In the most traditional of these busy restaurants, where there might be a hundred different dishes on any given day, you don't order. A specific meze, left to the chef's discretion, will arrive with your first round of tsipouro or ouzo. Another, different, perhaps more filling or more spicy, meze will arrive with the second round. As you linger, imbibe, and nibble, new and different mezethes are served, always one at a time, with each new round. If one meze is a small pie, the next one might be a pickled vegetable, followed by a dip or a bean dish or some fish. Variety, playfulness, and surprise are key.

The ritual of meze eating expresses itself in other ways, too, not so much according to the way restaurants have developed their menus, but according to the way people behave, their body language and mannerisms, while eating.

Once, for example, in a tiny fishing village on the island of Sifnos, I had descended with a group of friends to a place we were told had really fresh fish. The place was a picturesque hovel with two gas burners and tables whose legs were damp and rough because the sea washed right up onto them. In one corner, under a canopy of reeds and bramble put together to keep the piercing sun out, sat two of the owner's friends. They seemed permanently tanned, apparently from working under the Greek island sun for so many years. They were dressed in the well-worn kind of clothing that villagers never throw away, oblivious to the ephemera of fashions. They were also engrossed in a lengthy debate. One sat with his back to the wall with his right forearm resting on the table. This is the meze pose par excellence. Occasionally, he'd pick up his glass with his left hand, and use his fork to jab at a few slivers of fish that were fanned out on a plain white plate. His companion sat across from him, his back also against the wall, with his left arm on the table. Over the course of the two hours or so that we were there, they poured each other a few shots of ouzo from a small glass carafe, and they picked occasionally at the few things that the owner had brought for them to eat: four cucumber sticks; *tsiros*, air-dried small anchovies and an island specialty; and a small square of feta with three olives on the side. There was a little bread, too.

This is a scene I have witnessed so many times in so many small, forgotten places that I have come to realize that body language is as much a part of meze culture as the choice of simple dishes and strong, unctuous drinks. At a traditional meze meal, you don't sit facing the table, but rather facing the world and abutting the table with one side of your body. Why? According to my friend Zouraris, because it's not supposed to be a proper meal. The focus is on the social, on the conversation, on the exchange of opinions. Food is there just to facilitate that.

That is not to say, of course, that the food doesn't matter at all. Some of the best food in Greece, indeed in the whole eastern Aegean, is on the meze table.

Because they are meant to tease, the best mezethes have an element of wit and allure. Some of the most naturally attractive dishes in Greece are mezethes. They tend to be colorful without necessarily being artful so texture and variety are important. An array of mezethes should include soft spreads; crunchy, fried, or crisp baked foods; and both hot and cold dishes.

There is an element of fun in mezethes. This is lighthearted eating, a savory flirtation that can be indulgent just because it is not supposed to be very serious.

Mezethes have to have a certain snappy spirit. There are lots of wrapped, individual dishes; small hand-held pies; spicy, robust dips; crunchy fried foods; luscious baked dishes oozing with melted cheese; garlicky seafood and aromatic grilled meats. For an American cook, mezethes make perfect party food, excellent brunch fare, and natural offerings for buffet feasts.

The dishes in this book run the gamut of meze fare. Most come from the traditional Greek table, but some are culled from nearby traditions, such as Turkish and Lebanese cuisine. Some are modern versions of older dishes. All are accessible and can be prepared in American kitchens.

# HOW TO PUT TOGETHER A MEZE SPREAD ✳

A meze spread is not meant to be a meal, but a nosh, a communal, convivial landscape of small and varied dishes perfect for grazing. Some offerings on the table might be store-bought, such as olives, cheeses, cured fish, or thin slices of spicy pastourma, the cured beef so well loved in the eastern Mediterranean. Pita bread or any of the Middle Eastern flat breads now available in the United States, as well as good-quality country-style bread, should also be on the table.

There is no hard-and-fast rule regarding what dishes work best together for a meze spread, but variety—in textures, flavors, colors, temperatures, and types of food—is crucial. There has to be a little of everything, from creamy dips to golden, crisp phyllo pastries, to refreshing salads to juicy meatballs or vegetable fritters, to one or two fish or seafood dishes, and richer dishes in small portions gushing with cheese and sauce. When composing menus based upon mezethes, a sense of variety and balance is the most important thing to keep in mind.

# WHAT TO DRINK WITH MEZETHES ✳

Mezethes are meant to be served with alcohol, either wine or headier spirits such as ouzo, Greek tsipouro, and raki (grape distillates like eau-de-vie and grappa), and Turkish arak.

# MATCHING MEZETHES TO GREEK WINES ✳

Greek wines have come a long way from bulk retsina. In the last decade they have gained wide recognition across Europe, especially in the prestigious British market, and they are finally making their way across the Atlantic. I wanted to provide general guidelines for pairing certain types of mezethes with Greek wines, and at the back of the book I offer a list of sites and contacts for finding fine Greek wines in the United States.

There are over three hundred indigenous grape varietals in Greece and two major trends in Greek wine making: Some wines are made exclusively with the noble, indigenous Greek varietals and others are blends of Greek grapes and well-known international grapes, such as Cabernet Sauvignon, Merlot, Syrah, and Chardonnay.

The majority of Greek wines, whether blends or not, are meant to be drunk with robust Greek cuisine, so they make natural partners for mezethes. You could, in fact, choose a wine first, and then go on to make a selection of mezethes to accompany it.

The two major red grape varietals in Greece are the xynomavro (xee-NO-ma-vro) from Naoussa in Macedonia and the agiorgitiko (A-ee-or-GHEE-tee-ko), or St. George, from Nemea in the Peloponnisos. The xynomavro is one of the most difficult grapes to master. It is believed to be the ancestor of the Nebiolo grape of the Piedmont, and it produces wines that are tannic when young and extremely complex when aged. A good xynomavro will have an intriguing nose, redolent of black olive, anise, leather, tobacco, oregano, rosemary, and thyme. A light xynomavro matches up very well to many of the egg dishes in this book, as well as with recipes that call for sun-dried or stewed tomatoes, especially when coupled with cheese, black olives, and foods that are redolent with Anatolian spices. Spicy meat dishes, recipes with pastourma, as well as cheese fritters, all go very well with xynomavro. I recommend xynomavro for almost all the kebab dishes as well as for the robust bean dishes.

The agiorgitiko wines, from Nemea in the Peloponnisos, are more giving and soft. You can often detect raspberry and other fruits in an agiorgitiko. These are good wines to match up with eggplant and with dishes rich in olive oil. They also go well with sweet and aromatic meat dishes, such as Spareribs Marinated in Wine, Honey, Star Anise, and Garlic (page 180) and Cinnamon-Scented Lamb Cubes with Tomatoes and Onions (page 181), and can hold their own against the strong aromas of pastourma, with its fenugreek-infused spice rub.

Greece produces many more white wines than reds, and here, too, single varietals and blends are equally savored. In general, most Greek whites tend to be acidic and citrusy and they go well with grilled fish and seafood.

Complex seafood dishes that are rich with olive oil, lemon juice, and garlic go very well with the wines from Mandineia in the central Peloponnisos, which are produced from the moschofilero (moss-ko-FEE-lai-ro) grape. The moschofilero is probably the most aromatic white wine grape, redolent of rose petals, with a beautiful, crisp finish. It goes very well with dishes that have mint and garlic, as well as with some of the seafood and cheese dishes such as saganaki.

Unctuous dips, such as taramosalata, and dishes whose main flavor component is sharp feta cheese go well with crisp, dry wines such as those made with the robolla (ro-BO-la) grape from Cephalonia or with the assyrtico (a-SEER-tee-ko) of Santorini. Both wines have a pleasant minerality. The robolla produces delicate, crisp wines with a lemon or citrus finish, whereas the assyrtico, truly one of the world's most unique grapes, grown on Santorini's volcanic soil, produces crisp, bone-dry wines with beautiful acidity. Most of the octopus dishes in this book are a perfect match for wines made from the assyrtico grape. Robolla or assyrtico wines also match up well with spinach and cheese combinations, such as the Spinach and Three-Cheese Triangles (page 72) and the Potatoes Stuffed with Spinach, Dill, and Cheese (page 130). The sardine dishes (pages 151, 154, 156, and 157) also pair up well to these two crisp island wines.

Another major Greek white grape varietal is the roditis (Ro-DEE-tees), which is produced in the northern and western parts of the Peloponnisos. The roditis produces wines that have a grassy, herbal quality and go great with almost all the salads here as well as with dishes that call for crisp green vegetables such as asparagus.

## RETSINA

No mention of what to drink with mezethes would be complete without a tip of the hat to retsina, the distinct, resonated white or rose wine that is both embraced and shunned by wine lovers.

For decades, retsina was synonymous with Greek wines, especially with mass-produced bulk wines of inferior quality. Among an older generation of Greeks, retsina is still popular, but it has lost ground to the new, sophisticated, very well-made Greek wines that mark the industry today.

But even in the world of retsina, revolutions take foot, and there has been one quietly going on ever since a brash young wine maker named Yiannis Paraskevopoulos developed an upscale, crisp retsina with barely a trace of pine resin and a crisp, clean character. Many wine makers are now experimenting with Greece's most traditional wine, and many new retsinas are starting to appear. These have nothing to do with the bulk wines of yore. An interesting light retsina is also produced by the well-known Greek wine maker Tsantalis.

The truth is that retsina is oftentimes the perfect match for robust mezethes, and one of the few wines that can stand up to many of the garlic-flavored dishes that Greeks like so much on the meze table.

## SPIRITS

With the exception of the sweeter meat dishes and some of the more delicate fish and seafood dishes, all the recipes in this book can be matched with ouzo or with the grape distillates tsipouro and raki.

Mezethes and ouzo, the anise-flavored spirit that clouds up when you add ice or water, have always been perfect partners. Ditto for tsipouro and raki. Greeks have always made grape distillates similar to the Italian grappa, and in the last few years a few very talented distillers and wine makers have been producing fine quality distillates from single grape varietals. These, too, are increasingly available in the United States.

# Vegetarian Platter

1 large hothouse cucumber

2 teaspoons red wine vinegar

1 medium, firm, ripe tomato

1 boiled potato, peeled and quartered

1/2 cup extra virgin olive oil

Salt and freshly ground black pepper to taste

1 teaspoon dried Greek oregano

Juice of 1/2 lemon

2 hard-boiled eggs, quartered

2 pita bread rounds, cut into wedges

1/2 cup Tangy Yogurt with Sautéed Carrots and Mint (page 14)

1/2 cup classic Greek feta cheese spread (page 24)

8 cracked green olives

4 to 6 pickled peperoncini peppers

I. Peel the cucumber and cut in half across its width. Cut each piece in half again, lengthwise, then cut into 3 strips, about as thick as a woman's index finger. Salt and toss with vinegar.

2. Cut the tomato into 8 wedges.

3. Cut the potato in half across the width, then in half again lengthwise. Toss with 2 tablespoons of the olive oil, the salt, pepper, 1/2 teaspoon of the oregano, and the lemon juice.

4. Place the cucumber, tomato, potato, and egg quarters decoratively around a medium serving platter or large plate, alternating between each. Spoon the tangy yogurt in the center to one side, place the olives next to it, and then spoon the cheese spread next to that. Place the pickled peppers around the platter.

5. Toast the pita bread wedges lightly, or brush them with 2 tablespoons olive oil and bake in a preheated 350°F oven for about 7 minutes, turning once, until warmed through and lightly browned. Tuck the pita wedges on the periphery of the platter, under the raw vegetables.

6. Drizzle the remaining olive oil over the vegetables. Season with additional salt, pepper, and the remaining oregano, and serve.

# Seafood Meze Platter

Use the vegetarian meze platter as the foundation, but omit the tzatziki and the boiled potato. Embellish the vegetarian platter with:

**MAKES 6 TO 8 SERVINGS**

**6 to 8 panfried jumbo shrimp (page 141)**

**6 to 8 Batter-Fried Mussels (page 110)**

**2 octopus tentacles, from the octopus with herbs (page 162), cut into 1-inch chunks**

**4 to 6 pieces marinated anchovies (page 152) or 4 to 6 pieces salted sardine fillets**

**10 to 12 Greek fries (page 98)(one potato, fried)**

**¹/₂ cup taramosalata (page 27), in lieu of tzatziki**

# Meat Meze Platter

Use the vegetarian platter as the foundation, but without the boiled potato. Embellish it with:

**4 TO 6 GREEK MEATBALLS, PAGE 172**

**1 Greek or other spicy sausage, grilled and cut into chunks, or 1 small dried sausage, cut into 1-inch rounds**

**2 slices smoked ham, trimmed, halved, and rolled up into small cylinders**

**4 to 6 chunks Greek kasseri cheese**

**4 to 6 pieces sesame-covered feta saganaki (page 104)**

**4 to 6 slices fried preserved peppers or breaded, fried hot peppers**

# DIPS, SPREADS, AND RELISHES

You have to understand the place bread holds in the heart and palate of a typical Greek to understand why the cuisine brims with so many different kinds of dips and spreads, in essence, relishes.

The practice of marrying bread with some sort of relish, and the practice of using bread as a utensil with which to gather up the relish, goes back to the farthest reaches of antiquity. It is a custom that remains embedded in the national psyche.

Relishes take the form of pungent dips and spreadable "salads," such as roasted eggplant salad—melitzanosalata—and fish-roe salad, taramosalata. Many of these colorful, robust dishes are among the best-known Greek food, fun to eat, and always present on restaurant menus in every dining category.

I decided not to include the absolute classics here, such as tzatziki, the well-known Greek dip made with yogurt, cucumbers, and garlic, and standard skordalia, made with potatoes or bread and garlic. You can find those recipes in every Greek cookbook, including my own previous ones. I opted to present dishes that don't stray that far from the classic fare but have a twist—for example, tzatziki made with sautéed carrots and mint, inspired by a Turkish meze; several versions of roasted eggplant salad, because eggplant is so versatile. Many of the recipes here are regional variations on the classics.

Almost every dip, spread, and relish on the meze table is turbocharged with flavor, from unsparing amounts of garlic to cayenne pepper to lemon. Their pungency is a welcome foil to the mild taste of bread, with which most are savored, and a counter to the strong liqueurs that these dips and spreads are usually meant to accompany. They make excellent party fare, and are easily matched with all sorts of other foods, such as bean dishes, roasted meats, grilled or panfried seafood, and more.

# Spicy Tomato–Pepper Relish

The key to making this simple dish well is in the chopping. All ingredients should be cut into a fine dice, smaller than confetti but not so small that the pieces are indiscernible. This relish is a salad of sorts in that it contains a mixture of fresh, chopped vegetables, but it is eaten more like a salsa, scooped up with or spooned onto a piece of crisp pita bread. The dish is a classic in Greece's many kebab houses and goes well with grilled meats and chicken.

**MAKES 6 TO 8 SERVINGS**

**2 large tomatoes, peeled, seeded, and finely diced**

**1 to 3 fresh chile peppers to taste, seeded and minced**

**2 medium red bell peppers, seeded and finely diced**

**2 medium green bell peppers, seeded and finely diced**

**1 medium red onion, finely chopped**

**2 large garlic cloves, minced**

**¼ cup extra virgin Greek olive oil**

**3 tablespoons good-quality tomato paste**

**Juice of 1 large lemon**

**Salt to taste**

**Cayenne pepper to taste**

Combine the first 6 ingredients. In a small bowl, vigorously mix together the olive oil, tomato paste, and lemon juice. Season with salt and cayenne. Mix the paste into the fresh ingredients. Transfer the mixture to a bowl, cover, and refrigerate for at least 2 hours and up to 6 hours before serving. Serve either cool or at room temperature.

# Tangy Yogurt with Sautéed Carrots and Mint

This refreshing dipping sauce takes its cue from the Turkish yogurt dip *haintari*. In Greece it is often served in kebab houses and mezethopoleia run by Anatolian Greeks. The flavors are very robust. Serve the dip alone with toasted pita wedges, with ground meat dishes such as the ground lamb skewers (page 182), or with either of the two meatball recipes (pages 170 and 172).

**MAKES 4 TO 6 SERVINGS**

⅓ cup extra virgin Greek olive oil

2 medium carrots, shredded

3 garlic cloves, finely chopped

⅓ cup fresh mint leaves, cut into very thin strips (julienne)

2 cups thick Greek or Mediterranean-style yogurt or drained plain yogurt (see Note on page 51)

Salt to taste

2 to 3 tablespoons lemon juice to taste

Paprika

Fresh mint leaves for garnish

**1.** Heat 2 tablespoons of the olive oil in a nonstick skillet over medium heat and cook the carrots, stirring, until soft, about 10 minutes. Add the garlic and mint, and stir for a minute until the garlic softens and the mint wilts.

**2.** Place the yogurt in a mixing bowl. Add the cooked carrot mixture, salt, the remaining olive oil, and lemon juice. Place in the refrigerator, covered, for 1 hour and serve garnished with a sprinkling of paprika and the mint leaves.

# Spicy Carrot Puree with Mint-Flavored Yogurt

MAKES 6 TO 8 SERVINGS

**FOR THE CARROTS**

**4 large carrots, chopped**

**½ teaspoon cumin seeds**

**1 teaspoon caraway seeds**

**2 to 3 tablespoons extra virgin olive oil**

**2 tablespoons fresh lemon juice**

**Salt and cayenne pepper or hot paprika to taste**

**FOR THE YOGURT**

**½ cup thick Greek or Mediterranean-style yogurt or drained plain yogurt (see Note on page 51)**

**1 tablespoon extra virgin olive oil to taste**

**1 tablespoon fresh lemon juice**

**3 garlic cloves, peeled**

**Salt to taste**

**2 tablespoons fresh mint leaves cut into very thin strips (julienne)**

1. Place the carrots in a vegetable steamer in a medium pot with about 2 inches of water, cover, and steam over medium heat until soft, about 25 minutes.

2. Pound the cumin and caraway seeds together in a mortar and pestle.

3. When the carrots are soft, transfer to a food processor and pulse once or twice for a few seconds, to mash. Add 2 tablespoons olive oil, lemon juice, salt, and spices, and pulse a few more times to puree until smooth.

4. Place the carrot mixture on a serving dish and make a well in the center.

5. Mix together the yogurt, olive oil, and lemon juice. Crush the garlic cloves in the mortar with a little salt and add this to the yogurt. Season to taste with additional salt. Place in the center of the plate, sprinkle with the mint leaves, and serve.

VARIATION

Instead of the yogurt, try serving the carrot puree with a dollop of the whipped basil–lemon feta (page 22), or with a dollop of Spicy Whipped Feta (page 24).

# Garlicky Yogurt Dip with Dried Apricots

This is one of my favorite combinations in the world. The origin of the dish is Turkish, but it is found in Greece, a rare treat almost always prepared by Anatolian Greek cooks. It is a wonderful accompaniment to kebabs and meatballs.

**MAKES 6 TO 8 SERVINGS**

2 cups thick Greek or Mediterranean-style yogurt or drained plain yogurt (see Note on page 51)

8 to 10 dried apricots to taste, finely chopped

3 garlic cloves, finely chopped

Salt to taste

Combine all the ingredients in a serving bowl and chill for 1 hour, covered. Serve immediately.

# Roasted Eggplant Dip with Walnuts, Coriander Seeds, and Scallions

The Greek love affair with the eggplant knows no end. There are dozens of eggplant salads, dips, and spreads. Every taverna, every homey restaurant, every good cook has his or her own rendition and favorite. So many of them are good that I have opted to include a few here. The eggplant is perhaps the world's most versatile vegetable. Try serving this with some of the baked sardine dishes (pages 151 and 156), with the panfried shrimp (page 141), or with one of my personal favorites, the "breaded" sardines on page 157.

---

**MAKES ABOUT 2 CUPS,**

**OR ENOUGH FOR 6 SERVINGS**

**2 medium eggplants, about ½ pound each**

**⅔ cup shelled walnuts**

**2 teaspoons coriander seeds**

**3 tablespoons fresh lemon juice**

**3 scallions, roots and tough upper greens removed, sliced into thin rings**

**⅔ cup extra virgin olive oil, preferably Greek**

**Salt to taste**

**½ to 1 teaspoon sugar to taste (optional)**

---

1. Wash and pat dry the eggplants. Keep the stems intact. Roast the eggplants over a low open flame directly on top of the stove. Alternatively, you may roast them under the broiler, about 6 inches away from the heat source. Turn occasionally so that the eggplants roast evenly on all sides. They are done when their skins are charred all around and when they are tender to the touch, especially near the dense stem end. Remove from the flame and place on a cutting board.

2. While the eggplants are roasting, pulverize the walnuts and coriander seeds together in a food processor until they reach a coarse, mealy consistency.

3. To remove the eggplant pulp: Hold the eggplant from the stem end. Using a sharp paring knife, slit the first eggplant lengthwise down the middle. Use the body of the egg-

plant as your guide, and with the knife cut away the skin over both halves, as you would when removing the crust from a loaf of bread. The stem and eggplant pulp should be left, with the charred skin peeled away and fallen to the surface of the cutting board. Score the pulp lengthwise as well as crosswise to facilitate its removal. Using the knife or a spoon, remove as much of the seed mass as possible. Remove the pulp and place it in the bowl of the food processor. Pour the lemon juice over it.

4. Save 2 tablespoons of the scallions for garnish. Add the rest to the food processor bowl. Pulse on and off once or twice to combine. Add the oil in $1/3$-cup increments, and pulse to combine well. Taste the eggplant as you go. Season with salt. If the eggplant is bitter, add a little sugar. Remove to a serving dish. Garnish with the remaining scallions and serve.

## NOTE

The eggplant dip may be made several hours ahead and kept, covered, in the refrigerator. Garnish just before serving.

# Roasted Eggplant Salad with Feta, Onion, Peppers, and Garlic

I first tasted this lovely appetizer at one of my favorite Athenian haunts, the Naxos Cafeneion in Psyrri, a once industrial part of downtown Athens that has become chic and hip. The Cafeneion predates the neighborhood's gentrification and is still a place where Greek islanders come to socialize. On Sunday afternoons the scene is a madhouse. This simple eggplant salad is on every table, a much-liked classic for people to dip into while they wait, and wait, for the rest of the meal to arrive.

---

**MAKES ABOUT 4 CUPS,**
**OR ENOUGH FOR 8 TO 10 SERVINGS**

**3 large eggplants, about 10 ounces each**

**Juice of 1 large lemon**

**½ cup extra virgin Greek olive oil**

**1 large red onion, finely chopped**

**2 medium green bell peppers, finely chopped**

**3 garlic cloves, minced**

**1¼ cups (about 7½ ounces) Greek feta, crumbled**

**Salt and freshly ground black pepper to taste**

**½ teaspoon cayenne pepper**

---

1. Wash and pat dry the eggplants. Keep the stems intact. Roast the eggplants over a low open flame directly on top of the stove. Alternatively, you may roast them under the broiler, about 6 inches away from the heat source. Turn occasionally so that the eggplants roast evenly on all sides. They are done when their skins are charred all around and when they are tender to the touch, especially near the dense stem end. Remove from the flame and place on a cutting board.

2. Using a sharp paring knife, slit the first eggplant lengthwise down the middle. Using the body of the eggplant as your guide, with the knife cut away the skin over both halves, the way you would when removing the crust from a loaf of bread. The stem and egg-

plant pulp should be left, with the charred skin peeled away and fallen to the surface of the cutting board. Score the pulp lengthwise as well as crosswise to facilitate its removal. Using the knife or a teaspoon, remove as much of the seed mass as possible. Remove the pulp and place it in a mixing bowl.

3. Squeeze the lemon juice over the pulp and toss quickly. Add the olive oil and stir the eggplant into the oil with a fork until all the oil is absorbed. Do not mash the eggplant with the fork.

4. Add the chopped vegetables and feta, and toss to combine well. Season with salt, pepper, and cayenne. Serve immediately.

# Feta Whipped with Basil, Lemon, and Pepper

Feta is the Greek culinary answer to everything. Greek cooks savor their national cheese on its own, but more often than not use it as the base for myriad dips and spreads, or in fillings, stuffings, and gratins. This recipe is a not-so-classic rendition of the time-honored feta cheese spread called *htipiti*. It calls for basil, which Greeks do not use as readily as mint and oregano. You can use the dip as a filling for peppers, too. Try stuffing raw green or red peppers with the mix, refrigerating until the cheese firms up, and then cutting the peppers into rounds.

---

**MAKES ABOUT 3 CUPS,
OR ENOUGH FOR 8 TO 10 SERVINGS**

**3 cups (about 12 ounces) crumbled feta, preferably Greek**

**3 scant tablespoons dried basil**

**1 heaping teaspoon cracked black peppercorns**

**²/₃ cup extra virgin olive oil, preferably Greek**

**6 tablespoons fresh lemon juice**

**1 teaspoon lemon zest, cut into very thin strips (julienne)**

---

I. Pulse together the feta, basil, and pepper in a food processor until combined.

2. Add the olive oil and lemon juice, alternating between each and pulsing after each addition, until the mixture is dense but spreads easily. Remove to a serving plate, garnish with lemon zest, and serve.

NOTE

The dip may be made 2 to 3 hours ahead of time and kept, covered, in the refrigerator.